MAD LIBS®

GO TEAM! MAD LIBS

by

MAD LIBS
An imprint of Penguin Random House LLC, New York

First published in the United States of America by Mad Libs,
an imprint of Penguin Random House LLC, New York, 2022

Concept created by Roger Price & Leonard Stern

Cover illustration by Scott Brooks

Printed in the United States of America

ISBN 9780593384572
1 3 5 7 9 10 8 6 4 2
COMR

MAD LIBS®

INSTRUCTIONS

MAD LIBS® is a game for people who don't like games! It can be played by one, two, three, four, or forty.

• RIDICULOUSLY SIMPLE DIRECTIONS

In this tablet you will find stories containing blank spaces where words are left out. One player, the READER, selects one of these stories. The READER does not tell anyone what the story is about. Instead, he/she asks the other players, the WRITERS, to give him/her words. These words are used to fill in the blank spaces in the story.

• TO PLAY

The READER asks each WRITER in turn to call out a word—an adjective or a noun or whatever the space calls for—and uses them to fill in the blank spaces in the story. The result is a MAD LIBS® game.

When the READER then reads the completed MAD LIBS® game to the other players, they will discover that they have written a story that is fantastic, screamingly funny, shocking, silly, crazy, or just plain dumb—depending upon which words each WRITER called out.

• EXAMPLE (*Before* and *After*)

"__________________ !" he said __________________
EXCLAMATION ADVERB

as he jumped into his convertible __________________ and
NOUN

drove off with his __________________ wife.
ADJECTIVE

"OUCH !" he said HAPPILY
EXCLAMATION ADVERB

as he jumped into his convertible CAT and
NOUN

drove off with his BRAVE wife.
ADJECTIVE

MAD LIBS®

QUICK REVIEW

In case you have forgotten what adjectives, adverbs, nouns, and verbs are, here is a quick review:

An ADJECTIVE describes something or somebody. *Lumpy*, *soft*, *ugly*, *messy*, and *short* are adjectives.

An ADVERB tells how something is done. It modifies a verb and usually ends in "ly." *Modestly*, *stupidly*, *greedily*, and *carefully* are adverbs.

A NOUN is the name of a person, place, or thing. *Sidewalk*, *umbrella*, *bridle*, *bathtub*, and *nose* are nouns.

A VERB is an action word. *Run*, *pitch*, *jump*, and *swim* are verbs. Put the verbs in past tense if the directions say PAST TENSE. *Ran*, *pitched*, *jumped*, and *swam* are verbs in the past tense.

When we ask for A PLACE, we mean any sort of place: a country or city (*Spain*, *Cleveland*) or a room (*bathroom*, *kitchen*).

An EXCLAMATION or SILLY WORD is any sort of funny sound, gasp, grunt, or outcry, like *Wow!*, *Ouch!*, *Whomp!*, *Ick!*, and *Gadzooks!*

When we ask for specific words, like a NUMBER, a COLOR, an ANIMAL, or a PART OF THE BODY, we mean a word that is one of those things, like *seven*, *blue*, *horse*, or *head*.

When we ask for a PLURAL, it means more than one. For example, *cat* pluralized is *cats*.

MAD LIBS® is fun to play with friends, but you can also play it by yourself! To begin with, DO NOT look at the story on the page below. Fill in the blanks on this page with the words called for. Then, using the words you have selected, fill in the blank spaces in the story.

Now you've created your own hilarious MAD LIBS® game!

READY? OKAY!

PLURAL NOUN ____________

VERB ____________

EXCLAMATION ____________

ADJECTIVE ____________

PART OF THE BODY ____________

ADJECTIVE ____________

ADJECTIVE ____________

ADVERB ____________

NOUN ____________

VERB ____________

VERB ENDING IN "ING" ____________

ADJECTIVE ____________

SILLY WORD ____________

VERB ____________

VERB ____________

NOUN ____________

PART OF THE BODY (PLURAL) ____________

NOUN ____________

MAD LIBS

READY? OKAY!

We're the ______________ (PLURAL NOUN); say our name!

Are you ready to ______________ (VERB)? Because it's our game!

______________ (EXCLAMATION)! That's right—we're here to win!

Our team is so ______________ (ADJECTIVE), it'll make your ______________ (PART OF THE BODY) spin.

We're ______________ (ADJECTIVE) and we're ______________ (ADJECTIVE). We're the best in the land!

And you're gonna lose ______________ (ADVERB), just as planned.

We heard you think your ______________ (NOUN) is tough,

but when we ______________ (VERB), you'll have had enough!

Sorry—not sorry—that you're ______________ (VERB ENDING IN "ING") to lose.

We're so ______________ (ADJECTIVE) we're not in your shoes.

______________ (SILLY WORD)! There's just no other way

to say we're going to ______________ (VERB) today!

So don't even try to ______________ (VERB) up a fight.

Our team has all the ______________ (NOUN) and might!

Hang your ______________ (PART OF THE BODY (PLURAL)); admit we're great!

That's the ______________ (NOUN)—there's no debate!

MAD LIBS® is fun to play with friends, but you can also play it by yourself! To begin with, DO NOT look at the story on the page below. Fill in the blanks on this page with the words called for. Then, using the words you have selected, fill in the blank spaces in the story.

Now you've created your own hilarious MAD LIBS® game!

CHEERLEADING 101

ADJECTIVE ____________

VERB ENDING IN "ING" ____________

PART OF THE BODY (PLURAL) ____________

VERB ____________

NUMBER ____________

NOUN ____________

NOUN ____________

VERB (PAST TENSE) ____________

PART OF THE BODY (PLURAL) ____________

NOUN ____________

NOUN ____________

OCCUPATION ____________

PART OF THE BODY ____________

SOMETHING ALIVE (PLURAL) ____________

VERB (PAST TENSE) ____________

PLURAL NOUN ____________

VERB ENDING IN "ING" ____________

MAD LIBS®

CHEERLEADING 101

Here's a guide to some of the most ____________ (ADJECTIVE) ____________ (VERB ENDING IN "ING") terms:

- **Aerial:** a tumbling skill that is performed without your ____________ (PART OF THE BODY (PLURAL)) touching the ground; for example, a Basket ____________ (VERB) is a stunt involving ____________ (NUMBER) or more bases, two of whom toss the ____________ (NOUN) into the air
- **Candlesticks:** a/an ____________ (NOUN) where the arms are ____________ (VERB (PAST TENSE)) and the ____________ (PART OF THE BODY (PLURAL)) face each other
- **Dismount:** method used to return to a/an ____________ (NOUN) position following a/an ____________ (NOUN)
- **Inversion:** any stunt where the ____________ (OCCUPATION)'s feet are higher than their ____________ (PART OF THE BODY)
- **Mount:** any skill in which one or more ____________ (SOMETHING ALIVE (PLURAL)) are ____________ (VERB (PAST TENSE)) on top of each other
- **Stick:** to land a tumbling skill without taking extra ____________ (PLURAL NOUN) or to finish a stunt without ____________ (VERB ENDING IN "ING")

MAD LIBS® is fun to play with friends, but you can also play it by yourself! To begin with, DO NOT look at the story on the page below. Fill in the blanks on this page with the words called for. Then, using the words you have selected, fill in the blank spaces in the story.

Now you've created your own hilarious MAD LIBS® game!

PEP TALK

NUMBER ______

OCCUPATION (PLURAL) ______

PERSON IN ROOM ______

PLURAL NOUN ______

ADJECTIVE ______

ADJECTIVE ______

PART OF THE BODY ______

PLURAL NOUN ______

VERB ______

VERB (PAST TENSE) ______

VERB ______

PART OF THE BODY (PLURAL) ______

VERB ______

PART OF THE BODY ______

VERB ______

SAME PERSON IN ROOM ______

MAD LIBS

PEP TALK

Coach: Okay, squad! Today we have a special guest. I've asked one of the top-________ (NUMBER) ________ (OCCUPATION (PLURAL)) I know to give us some pointers about cheerleading. I'd like to introduce ________ (PERSON IN ROOM).

Cheer Expert: Hi! I'm here today to remind you that it's the little ________ (PLURAL NOUN) that count in cheerleading. Keep your motions ________ (ADJECTIVE) and snappy. Your arms should always be ________ (ADJECTIVE) and in front of your ________ (PART OF THE BODY); keep them stiff and your ________ (PLURAL NOUN) tight. And ________ (VERB) those elbows—they should always be ________ (VERB (PAST TENSE)). ________ (VERB) your shoulders; they should not be up by your ________ (PART OF THE BODY (PLURAL)). And, of course, make your ________ (VERB) and clap motions count! Your hands should be under your ________ (PART OF THE BODY).

Coach: All right, squad! Let's ________ (VERB) the floor and show ________ (SAME PERSON IN ROOM) what we've got!

MAD LIBS® is fun to play with friends, but you can also play it by yourself! To begin with, DO NOT look at the story on the page below. Fill in the blanks on this page with the words called for. Then, using the words you have selected, fill in the blank spaces in the story.

Now you've created your own hilarious MAD LIBS® game!

S-P-I-R-I-T!

EXCLAMATION ______________________

PLURAL NOUN ______________________

VERB ______________________

VERB ______________________

ADJECTIVE ______________________

NOUN ______________________

TYPE OF FOOD ______________________

ADVERB ______________________

NOUN ______________________

SILLY WORD ______________________

VERB ______________________

NOUN ______________________

EXCLAMATION ______________________

VERB ______________________

VERB ______________________

LETTER OF THE ALPHABET ______________________

MAD LIBS®

S-P-I-R-I-T!

We've got spirit! Oh ______________ , we do!
EXCLAMATION

We have lots more ______________ than you!
PLURAL NOUN

We've got spirit! We ______________ and shout!
VERB

We're going to ______________ you—there's no doubt!
VERB

We've got spirit! We're ______________ and tough!
ADJECTIVE

Your ______________ is like a soft ______________ puff!
NOUN TYPE OF FOOD

We've got spirit! We ______________ back down!
ADVERB

We are the toughest ______________ around!
NOUN

We've got spirit! ______________ , let's hear!
SILLY WORD

It's time to ______________ it up a gear!
VERB

We've got spirit! You've got none!

The ______________ is over! And ______________ , we've won!
NOUN EXCLAMATION

We'll ______________ it again: We've got spirit!
VERB

We'll ______________ it out so you can hear it,
VERB

S-P-I-R-I- ______________ !
LETTER OF THE ALPHABET

MAD LIBS® is fun to play with friends, but you can also play it by yourself! To begin with, DO NOT look at the story on the page below. Fill in the blanks on this page with the words called for. Then, using the words you have selected, fill in the blank spaces in the story.

Now you've created your own hilarious MAD LIBS® game!

HIT THAT JUMP!

FIRST NAME ____________

VERB ENDING IN "ING" ____________

PLURAL NOUN ____________

VERB ____________

NOUN ____________

VERB ____________

ADJECTIVE ____________

LETTER OF THE ALPHABET ____________

ADJECTIVE ____________

ANIMAL ____________

VERB (PAST TENSE) ____________

PLURAL NOUN ____________

PART OF THE BODY ____________

VERB (PAST TENSE) ____________

ADJECTIVE ____________

NOUN ____________

VERB ____________

PART OF THE BODY ____________

MAD LIBS®

HIT THAT JUMP!

Hey, all you cheerleaders! It's ______________ (FIRST NAME) Herkimer here—grandfather of modern ______________ (VERB ENDING IN "ING"). Today, I'm going to talk to you about cheerleading ______________ (PLURAL NOUN). If you can ______________ (VERB) these, then you're bound to make it onto the ______________ (NOUN) and be there to ______________ (VERB) your team to VICTORY! Start with the ______________ (ADJECTIVE) jumps: the tuck jump; the ______________ (LETTER OF THE ALPHABET), also known as the ______________ (ADJECTIVE) jump; and the spread-______________ (ANIMAL). Once you have ______________ (VERB (PAST TENSE)) those, you can move on to more difficult ______________ (PLURAL NOUN), such as the ______________ (PART OF THE BODY)-touch; the hurdler, which can be ______________ (VERB (PAST TENSE)) to the front or the side; and the most ______________ (ADJECTIVE): the pike. And, of course, don't forget the ______________ (NOUN) that I invented: the herkie! Remember to ______________ (VERB) one arm straight up and have the other arm on your ______________ (PART OF THE BODY)!

MAD LIBS® is fun to play with friends, but you can also play it by yourself! To begin with, DO NOT look at the story on the page below. Fill in the blanks on this page with the words called for. Then, using the words you have selected, fill in the blank spaces in the story.

Now you've created your own hilarious MAD LIBS® game!

STUNT STYLE

VERB ____________________

ADJECTIVE ____________________

VERB ____________________

PART OF THE BODY ____________________

NOUN ____________________

VERB (PAST TENSE) ____________________

NOUN ____________________

PART OF THE BODY (PLURAL) ____________________

VERB ____________________

ADJECTIVE ____________________

NOUN ____________________

VERB ____________________

NOUN ____________________

PART OF THE BODY (PLURAL) ____________________

VERB ____________________

MAD LIBS®

STUNT STYLE

Flyer: Okay, we have got to ____________ (VERB) our stunts. As Coach always tells us, "____________ (ADJECTIVE) work will pay off."

Base #1: We've got the shoulder ____________ (VERB) and ____________ (PART OF THE BODY) stand down. But we need to work on our ____________ (NOUN) toss.

Base #2: We haven't ____________ (VERB (PAST TENSE)) the ____________ (NOUN), either. I need to keep my ____________ (PART OF THE BODY (PLURAL)) tight.

Flyer: And I want to make sure we nail our ____________ (VERB)-and-go stunt, too. I'm feeling a bit ____________ (ADJECTIVE) on that one.

Base #1: That might be my ____________ (NOUN). I need to ____________ (VERB) my dip.

Base #2: And I need to sync my ____________ (NOUN) with you.

Spotter: You guys know I have your ____________ (PART OF THE BODY (PLURAL)). Let's ____________ (VERB) the mat and get practicing!

MAD LIBS® is fun to play with friends, but you can also play it by yourself! To begin with, DO NOT look at the story on the page below. Fill in the blanks on this page with the words called for. Then, using the words you have selected, fill in the blank spaces in the story.

Now you've created your own hilarious MAD LIBS® game!

DON'T QUIT! BE FIT!

VERB ______________

NOUN ______________

VERB ENDING IN "ING" ______________

ADJECTIVE ______________

PART OF THE BODY ______________

SAME PART OF THE BODY ______________

VERB ______________

NOUN ______________

VERB ENDING IN "ING" ______________

VERB (PAST TENSE) ______________

ADJECTIVE ______________

PART OF THE BODY ______________

LETTER OF THE ALPHABET ______________

NOUN ______________

VERB ENDING IN "ING" ______________

ADJECTIVE ______________

VERB ______________

MAD LIBS®

DON'T QUIT! BE FIT!

Do you want to ____________ (VERB) your cheerleading to new levels? The recipe for success is one part practice, two parts ____________ (NOUN), and three parts ____________ (VERB ENDING IN "ING"). Here are some exercises that will help you stay ____________ (ADJECTIVE) and strong:

- ____________ (PART OF THE BODY) **explosions:** This exercise helps with jump height and ____________ (SAME PART OF THE BODY) strength.
- **Push-ups:** If you need to, ____________ (VERB) with your knees on the ____________ (NOUN).
- ____________ (VERB ENDING IN "ING") **toe-touches:** Focus on keeping your toes ____________ (VERB (PAST TENSE)), your legs ____________ (ADJECTIVE), and your ____________ (PART OF THE BODY) upright.
- ____________ (LETTER OF THE ALPHABET) **-ups:** These are great for your ____________ (NOUN) muscles, which you need for stunting and ____________ (VERB ENDING IN "ING").

And, as with any exercise, start ____________ (ADJECTIVE) and ____________ (VERB) up!

MAD LIBS® is fun to play with friends, but you can also play it by yourself! To begin with, DO NOT look at the story on the page below. Fill in the blanks on this page with the words called for. Then, using the words you have selected, fill in the blank spaces in the story.

Now you've created your own hilarious MAD LIBS® game!

PRACTICE MAKES PERFECT

VERB ENDING IN "ING" ______________________

PART OF THE BODY (PLURAL) ______________________

ADJECTIVE ______________________

ADJECTIVE ______________________

VERB ______________________

VERB ENDING IN "ING" ______________________

NOUN ______________________

NOUN ______________________

ADJECTIVE ______________________

VERB ENDING IN "ING" ______________________

PLURAL NOUN ______________________

CELEBRITY ______________________

VERB ______________________

NOUN ______________________

NUMBER ______________________

VERB ______________________

VERB ______________________

COLOR (PLURAL) ______________________

MAD LIBS®

PRACTICE MAKES PERFECT

Cheerleading is so much more than ________________ (VERB ENDING IN "ING") up and down and screaming at the top of your ________________ (PART OF THE BODY (PLURAL)). Cheerleaders need to be fit, ____________ (ADJECTIVE), agile, enthusiastic, and, above all, ____________ (ADJECTIVE). And if you practice and ____________ (VERB) hard, you will be G-R-E-A-T! Make sure you work on your flexibility by ________________ (VERB ENDING IN "ING") daily. (Tip: You can do this while watching your favorite ____________ (NOUN) on TV.) Practice your motions and chants in front of a full-length ____________ (NOUN). It's the best way to make sure your moves are ____________ (ADJECTIVE) and snappy. Have a friend video you ________________ (VERB ENDING IN "ING") your routines so you can see where you need to make any ________________ (PLURAL NOUN). Don't forget your pipes! Just like ____________ (CELEBRITY), you've got to be able to ____________ (VERB) out your cheers. Hit a/an ____________ (NOUN) and have someone try to move it. Try to hold it for ten to ____________ (NUMBER) seconds. Doing this will help you ____________ (VERB) your motions stronger. And remember to ____________ (VERB)—make sure you are always flashing those pearly ____________ (COLOR (PLURAL))!

MAD LIBS® is fun to play with friends, but you can also play it by yourself! To begin with, DO NOT look at the story on the page below. Fill in the blanks on this page with the words called for. Then, using the words you have selected, fill in the blank spaces in the story.

Now you've created your own hilarious MAD LIBS® game!

CHEERLEADING TRIVIA

PART OF THE BODY ____________________

ADJECTIVE ____________________

PLURAL NOUN ____________________

VERB (PAST TENSE) ____________________

ADJECTIVE ____________________

A PLACE ____________________

ANIMAL (PLURAL) ____________________

VERB ____________________

LETTER OF THE ALPHABET ____________________

VERB ____________________

PLURAL NOUN ____________________

OCCUPATION (PLURAL) ____________________

NOUN ____________________

PERSON IN ROOM ____________________

NUMBER ____________________

PLURAL NOUN ____________________

MAD LIBS®

CHEERLEADING TRIVIA

You may know a back ____________ (PART OF THE BODY) -spring from a/an ____________ (ADJECTIVE) -off, but how well do you know your cheerleading ____________ (PLURAL NOUN)?

1. Which college cheerleading squad has ____________ (VERB (PAST TENSE)) the most ____________ (ADJECTIVE) championships? (a) The University of Kentucky, (b) The University of (the) ____________ (A PLACE)
2. The Navarro College ____________ (ANIMAL (PLURAL)) were the stars of which TV show? (a) *Cheer*, (b) ____________ (VERB)
3. Which ____________ (LETTER OF THE ALPHABET) -FL cheerleading squad was the first to ____________ (VERB) original dance ____________ (PLURAL NOUN)? (a) The Dallas Cowboys Cheerleaders, (b) The Dallas ____________ (OCCUPATION (PLURAL))
4. Which mega-superstar used to be a/an ____________ (NOUN) for Rochester Adams High School? (a) Madonna, (b) ____________ (PERSON IN ROOM)

If you answered *a* for all ____________ (NUMBER) questions, you've earned a place in the squad! If you chose mainly *b*'s, you'd better hand in your ____________ (PLURAL NOUN).

MAD LIBS® is fun to play with friends, but you can also play it by yourself! To begin with, DO NOT look at the story on the page below. Fill in the blanks on this page with the words called for. Then, using the words you have selected, fill in the blank spaces in the story.

Now you've created your own hilarious MAD LIBS® game!

P-R-I-D-E!

SILLY WORD ________________

VERB (PAST TENSE) ________________

EXCLAMATION ________________

VERB ________________

VERB (PAST TENSE) ________________

NOUN ________________

VERB ENDING IN "ING" ________________

VERB ________________

VERB ________________

VERB (PAST TENSE) ________________

NOUN ________________

SAME NOUN ________________

VERB (PAST TENSE) ________________

SILLY WORD ________________

NOUN ________________

NOUN ________________

P-R-I-D-E!

____________ —don't you know,
SILLY WORD

we've ____________ that pride!
VERB (PAST TENSE)

____________ —let's hear it,
EXCLAMATION

don't ____________ and hide!
VERB

We've ____________ that pride;
VERB (PAST TENSE)

our ____________ is the best!
NOUN

No use ____________;
VERB ENDING IN "ING"

you won't ____________ the test!
VERB

We'll ____________ it again;
VERB

we've ____________ that pride!
VERB (PAST TENSE)

You've got no ____________;
NOUN

____________ is on our side!
SAME NOUN

We've ____________ that pride;
VERB (PAST TENSE)

____________ —yes, we do!
SILLY WORD

Just face the ____________;
NOUN

your ____________ is through!
NOUN

MAD LIBS® is fun to play with friends, but you can also play it by yourself! To begin with, DO NOT look at the story on the page below. Fill in the blanks on this page with the words called for. Then, using the words you have selected, fill in the blank spaces in the story.

Now you've created your own hilarious MAD LIBS® game!

TUMBLING TIPS

ADJECTIVE ______________________

PLURAL NOUN ______________________

VERB ENDING IN "ING" ______________________

PLURAL NOUN ______________________

NOUN ______________________

PLURAL NOUN ______________________

ADJECTIVE ______________________

VERB ______________________

VERB ______________________

PLURAL NOUN ______________________

VERB ENDING IN "ING" ______________________

ADVERB ______________________

ADJECTIVE ______________________

VERB ______________________

NOUN ______________________

ADJECTIVE ______________________

MAD LIBS®

TUMBLING TIPS

Tumbling skills are a/an ______________ (ADJECTIVE) way to add flair and ______________ (PLURAL NOUN) to a routine. But it can be scary to try ______________ (VERB ENDING IN "ING") for the first time. Here are some tips to help you crush those ______________ (PLURAL NOUN):

- Do not tumble without a/an ______________ (NOUN) or a coach to supervise. Use specific equipment, such as mats and ______________ (PLURAL NOUN). They are ______________ (ADJECTIVE) tools to help ______________ (VERB) your skills.
- Always ______________ (VERB) before you do anything, as stretching helps prevent ______________ (PLURAL NOUN).
- Visualize yourself not only ______________ (VERB ENDING IN "ING") the skill, but doing it ______________ (ADVERB). Be ______________ (ADJECTIVE), but be confident! If you believe you can do it, then ______________ (VERB) hard and give it your ______________ (NOUN), and chances are you can.

So be safe, be ______________ (ADJECTIVE), and go for it!

MAD LIBS® is fun to play with friends, but you can also play it by yourself! To begin with, DO NOT look at the story on the page below. Fill in the blanks on this page with the words called for. Then, using the words you have selected, fill in the blank spaces in the story.

Now you've created your own hilarious MAD LIBS® game!

CHEERLEADING ON THE SCREEN

VERB (PAST TENSE) ____________

NUMBER ____________

PLURAL NOUN ____________

NOUN ____________

ADJECTIVE ____________

VERB ____________

NOUN ____________

VERB ____________

VERB (PAST TENSE) ____________

ANIMAL (PLURAL) ____________

VERB ENDING IN "ING" ____________

NOUN ____________

VERB (PAST TENSE) ____________

PLURAL NOUN ____________

VERB ENDING IN "ING" ____________

VERB ____________

PLURAL NOUN ____________

NOUN ____________

MAD LIBS

CHEERLEADING ON THE SCREEN

If you're a true cheerleader, then you've ____________ (VERB (PAST TENSE)) every show and movie about cheerleading more than ____________ (NUMBER) times. Because watching ____________ (PLURAL NOUN) battling it out on the ____________ (NOUN) or on the field never gets ____________ (ADJECTIVE). If you haven't watched the show ____________ (VERB), you've obviously been living under a/an ____________ (NOUN). Go ____________ (VERB) it right now! It may have only been ____________ (VERB (PAST TENSE)) for one season, but *Hell-* ____________ (ANIMAL (PLURAL)) is another must-see about the competitive world of ____________ (VERB ENDING IN "ING"). If you want a good ____________ (NOUN), then watch ____________ (VERB (PAST TENSE)) *Up!*—a hilarious movie about two high-school ____________ (PLURAL NOUN) who decide to skip football camp and go to ____________ (VERB ENDING IN "ING") camp instead. And, of course, you can never watch ____________ (VERB) *It On* too many times. It's the movie that set the bar for cheerleading ____________ (PLURAL NOUN). Remember: This is not a/an ____________ (NOUN); it's a cheerocracy!

MAD LIBS® is fun to play with friends, but you can also play it by yourself! To begin with, DO NOT look at the story on the page below. Fill in the blanks on this page with the words called for. Then, using the words you have selected, fill in the blank spaces in the story.

Now you've created your own hilarious MAD LIBS® game!

CHEERLEADING OATH

VERB ______________________

PERSON IN ROOM ______________________

PLURAL NOUN ______________________

ADJECTIVE ______________________

ADJECTIVE ______________________

NOUN ______________________

VERB ______________________

PART OF THE BODY (PLURAL) ______________________

VERB ______________________

TYPE OF LIQUID ______________________

NUMBER ______________________

VERB ______________________

NOUN ______________________

PLURAL NOUN ______________________

ADJECTIVE ______________________

PLURAL NOUN ______________________

ADVERB ______________________

LETTER OF THE ALPHABET ______________________

NOUN ______________________

MAD LIBS

CHEERLEADING OATH

I solemnly ______________ (VERB) that I, ______________ (PERSON IN ROOM), will do my good, better, best to carry out my ______________ (PLURAL NOUN) as a cheerleader. I will be kind and ______________ (ADJECTIVE) to others at all times. I promise to always bring ______________ (ADJECTIVE) energy and an optimistic ______________ (NOUN). I will always ______________ (VERB) and point my ______________ (PART OF THE BODY (PLURAL)). I will never ______________ (VERB), and I will give it all the ______________ (TYPE OF LIQUID), sweat, and cheers I have. I know that safety is my number- ______________ (NUMBER) priority, and I will never do anything to ______________ (VERB) myself or my squad. I will attend every cheer-related ______________ (NOUN), including practices, camps, ______________ (PLURAL NOUN), and competitions. I promise that my uniform will always be ______________ (ADJECTIVE) (including my ______________ (PLURAL NOUN)) and fit ______________ (ADVERB). I will maintain a/an ______________ (LETTER OF THE ALPHABET) average in all my classes. I pledge my honesty, best ______________ (NOUN), and devotion to my squad.

MAD LIBS® is fun to play with friends, but you can also play it by yourself! To begin with, DO NOT look at the story on the page below. Fill in the blanks on this page with the words called for. Then, using the words you have selected, fill in the blank spaces in the story.

Now you've created your own hilarious MAD LIBS® game!

F-I-G-H-T!

NOUN ____________________

VERB ENDING IN "ING" ____________________

COLOR ____________________

VERB (PAST TENSE) ____________________

VERB ____________________

ADJECTIVE ____________________

VERB ____________________

ADJECTIVE ____________________

VERB ____________________

SAME VERB ____________________

LETTER OF THE ALPHABET ____________________

LETTER OF THE ALPHABET ____________________

VERB ____________________

VERB ____________________

MAD LIBS®

F-I-G-H-T!

We are the ______________ that can't be beat,
NOUN

and ______________ you will be so sweet!
VERB ENDING IN "ING"

Our mighty team is super ______________ -hot;
COLOR

once we get ______________, we can't be stopped!
VERB (PAST TENSE)

We are going to ______________ you down,
VERB

because we're the most ______________ team around!
ADJECTIVE

FIGHT—FIGHT— ______________ is our battle cry;
VERB

don't be ______________ —we'll show you why!
ADJECTIVE

Because we ______________ fight in a way that's better;
VERB

______________ it with us, shout out each letter!
SAME VERB

F- ______________ -G- ______________ -T!
LETTER OF THE ALPHABET / LETTER OF THE ALPHABET

______________ it together, that spells "FIGHT"!
VERB

Say it again: FIGHT—FIGHT— ______________!
VERB

MAD LIBS® is fun to play with friends, but you can also play it by yourself! To begin with, DO NOT look at the story on the page below. Fill in the blanks on this page with the words called for. Then, using the words you have selected, fill in the blank spaces in the story.

Now you've created your own hilarious MAD LIBS® game!

IT'S ALL ABOUT THE POM-POMS

SILLY WORD ____________________

SAME SILLY WORD ____________________

VERB (PAST TENSE) ____________________

VERB ENDING IN "ING" ____________________

CELEBRITY ____________________

PERSON IN ROOM ____________________

OCCUPATION (PLURAL) ____________________

NOUN ____________________

ADJECTIVE ____________________

ADJECTIVE ____________________

NOUN ____________________

VERB (PAST TENSE) ____________________

ADJECTIVE ____________________

NOUN ____________________

PLURAL NOUN ____________________

VERB ENDING IN "ING" ____________________

ADVERB ____________________

MAD LIBS

IT'S ALL ABOUT THE POM-POMS

Whether you say "pom-poms" or "__________ (SILLY WORD) - __________ (SAME SILLY WORD)," a sideline cheerleader isn't fully __________ (VERB (PAST TENSE)) unless they have a pair. Cheerleaders first started __________ (VERB ENDING IN "ING") pom-poms in the 1930s, and the invention is usually credited to __________ (CELEBRITY). However, __________ (PERSON IN ROOM), who was the founder of the National __________ (OCCUPATION (PLURAL)) Association, actually holds the patent on the pom-pom. The first pom-poms were made from crepe or __________ (NOUN) paper. They were __________ (ADJECTIVE) and fell apart easily, plus they were __________ (ADJECTIVE) in the rain. It wasn't until 1965 that a vinyl or __________ (NOUN) version of the pom-pom was __________ (VERB (PAST TENSE)). Vinyl pom-poms were __________ (ADJECTIVE), easier to use, and lasted a lot longer. Today, you can get pom-poms in just about any shape, __________ (NOUN), and color. And remember—in order for your __________ (PLURAL NOUN) to last, you have to take good care of them. This includes __________ (VERB ENDING IN "ING") them regularly and storing them __________ (ADVERB).

MAD LIBS® is fun to play with friends, but you can also play it by yourself! To begin with, DO NOT look at the story on the page below. Fill in the blanks on this page with the words called for. Then, using the words you have selected, fill in the blank spaces in the story.

Now you've created your own hilarious MAD LIBS® game!

TOP OF THE PYRAMID

ADJECTIVE ____________________

VERB ENDING IN "ING" ____________________

NOUN ____________________

ADJECTIVE ____________________

VERB (PAST TENSE) ____________________

VERB ____________________

ADJECTIVE ____________________

VERB ____________________

PLURAL NOUN ____________________

VERB (PAST TENSE) ____________________

NOUN ____________________

PLURAL NOUN ____________________

NUMBER ____________________

VERB ENDING IN "ING" ____________________

NOUN ____________________

A PLACE ____________________

VERB ____________________

ADJECTIVE ____________________

MAD LIBS®

TOP OF THE PYRAMID

Two ____________ ADJECTIVE organizations host the most notable national ____________ VERB ENDING IN "ING" competitions: the National Cheerleaders ____________ NOUN and the ____________ ADJECTIVE Cheerleaders Association. The competitions ____________ VERB (PAST TENSE) by these two organizations require that teams receive a bid in order to ____________ VERB. This usually means that a team has won ____________ ADJECTIVE and regional competitions, qualifying them to ____________ VERB in the national competition. The NCA College Nationals bring together the absolute best cheerleading ____________ PLURAL NOUN in the country. They are usually ____________ VERB (PAST TENSE) in April, and teams must submit a qualifying ____________ NOUN. More than two hundred incredible ____________ PLURAL NOUN compete, and there are ____________ NUMBER different divisions. And, of course, there are the ____________ VERB ENDING IN "ING" World Championships, known as "Worlds." This international competition is hosted by the US All ____________ NOUN Federation and held in (the) ____________ A PLACE. So ____________ VERB hard, stay ____________ ADJECTIVE, and you and your squad might be lifting the trophy next year!

MAD LIBS® is fun to play with friends, but you can also play it by yourself! To begin with, DO NOT look at the story on the page below. Fill in the blanks on this page with the words called for. Then, using the words you have selected, fill in the blank spaces in the story.

Now you've created your own hilarious MAD LIBS® game!

WEAR IT WITH PRIDE!

LETTER OF THE ALPHABET ________________

ADJECTIVE ________________

VERB ________________

ADJECTIVE ________________

OCCUPATION ________________

PLURAL NOUN ________________

ADJECTIVE ________________

PLURAL NOUN ________________

NOUN ________________

PERSON IN ROOM ________________

VERB ________________

PLURAL NOUN ________________

VERB (PAST TENSE) ________________

NOUN ________________

NUMBER ________________

NUMBER ________________

MAD LIBS®

WEAR IT WITH PRIDE!

Cheerleader #1: OM- ______________ (LETTER OF THE ALPHABET)! I am so ______________ (ADJECTIVE). I hope I remembered to ______________ (VERB) my entire uniform.

Cheerleader #2: Well, as long as it's ______________ (ADJECTIVE). You know that our ______________ (OCCUPATION) hates it when our ______________ (PLURAL NOUN) aren't clean and smelling ______________ (ADJECTIVE).

Cheerleader #1: I've got my spankies, my top, my shoes, and my ______________ (PLURAL NOUN), but I don't have my ______________ (NOUN) for my ponytail.

Cheerleader #2: Don't worry. I'm sure ______________ (PERSON IN ROOM) has one that you can ______________ (VERB).

Cheerleader #1: I'm sure she does, but I like mine because it has extra ______________ (PLURAL NOUN).

Cheerleader #2: Well, hurry up and get ______________ (VERB (PAST TENSE)). Because if we're late to the ______________ (NOUN), you know we'll have to do ______________ (NUMBER) push-ups and ______________ (NUMBER) burpees!

MAD LIBS® is fun to play with friends, but you can also play it by yourself! To begin with, DO NOT look at the story on the page below. Fill in the blanks on this page with the words called for. Then, using the words you have selected, fill in the blank spaces in the story.

Now you've created your own hilarious MAD LIBS® game!

FIRED UP!

ADJECTIVE ____________________

NOUN ____________________

TYPE OF EVENT (PLURAL) ____________________

VERB ____________________

ADJECTIVE ____________________

PLURAL NOUN ____________________

ADJECTIVE ____________________

VERB ____________________

SILLY WORD ____________________

PLURAL NOUN ____________________

VERB ____________________

NOUN ____________________

EXCLAMATION ____________________

NOUN ____________________

PERSON IN ROOM ____________________

NOUN ____________________

MAD LIBS®

FIRED UP!

We're fired up; we're ______________ hot!
(ADJECTIVE)

We bring the ______________; we will not stop!
(NOUN)

When it comes to ______________________, we can't be beat!
(TYPE OF EVENT (PLURAL))

Let me hear you ______________; get on your feet!
(VERB)

We are ______________; we are supreme!
(ADJECTIVE)

We've got the ________________ to beat your team!
(PLURAL NOUN)

Our team is ______________, so move aside!
(ADJECTIVE)

We're going to ______________ you on a ride!
(VERB)

______________, wait a minute!
(SILLY WORD)

Our team always puts some ________________ in it!
(PLURAL NOUN)

You better ______________ it; you're going down!
(VERB)

Because our ______________ is the best in town!
(NOUN)

________________! We bring the fight!
(EXCLAMATION)

You've got no ______________ against our might!
(NOUN)

Hey, ______________, don't you mess
(PERSON IN ROOM)

with our ______________; we are the best!
(NOUN)

MAD LIBS® is fun to play with friends, but you can also play it by yourself! To begin with, DO NOT look at the story on the page below. Fill in the blanks on this page with the words called for. Then, using the words you have selected, fill in the blank spaces in the story.

Now you've created your own hilarious MAD LIBS® game!

DON'T FORGET THE MASCOT!

ANIMAL ____________

OCCUPATION ____________

NOUN ____________

VERB ____________

VERB (PAST TENSE) ____________

TYPE OF EVENT ____________

NOUN ____________

VERB ENDING IN "ING" ____________

NOUN ____________

PLURAL NOUN ____________

ADVERB ____________

PLURAL NOUN ____________

ADJECTIVE ____________

NUMBER ____________

PART OF THE BODY ____________

VERB ENDING IN "ING" ____________

VERB ____________

NOUN ____________

MAD LIBS®

DON'T FORGET THE MASCOT!

Whether it's a purple ______________ (ANIMAL) or a giant ______________ (OCCUPATION), mascots are an important part of a cheerleading ______________ (NOUN)! The mascot will ______________ (VERB) the crowd before a game, get everyone ______________ (VERB (PAST TENSE)) up during the game, and definitely entertain the crowd during a/an ______________ (TYPE OF EVENT). A mascot is like a good-luck ______________ (NOUN) and embodies the ______________ (VERB ENDING IN "ING") spirit of a school and its team. Mascots represent a school's ______________ (NOUN), and ______________ (PLURAL NOUN) and fans will remember them ______________ (ADVERB) for the rest of their lives! But don't think that a mascot's job is all fun and ______________ (PLURAL NOUN)—it's ______________ (ADJECTIVE) work! A mascot's costume can weigh up to ______________ (NUMBER) pounds, and it's not that easy to see out of that over-size ______________ (PART OF THE BODY), especially while you're ______________ (VERB ENDING IN "ING") up and down. So when you see the mascot ______________ (VERB) the floor or the field, make sure to give them a big ______________ (NOUN)!

MAD LIBS® is fun to play with friends, but you can also play it by yourself! To begin with, DO NOT look at the story on the page below. Fill in the blanks on this page with the words called for. Then, using the words you have selected, fill in the blank spaces in the story.

Now you've created your own hilarious MAD LIBS® game!

BET YOU DIDN'T KNOW THAT!

ADJECTIVE ____________

VERB ENDING IN "ING" ____________

PERSON IN ROOM ____________

NOUN ____________

A PLACE ____________

NOUN ____________

VERB ENDING IN "ING" ____________

A PLACE ____________

PLURAL NOUN ____________

ADJECTIVE ____________

VERB (PAST TENSE) ____________

NUMBER ____________

NUMBER ____________

LETTER OF THE ALPHABET ____________

NOUN ____________

MAD LIBS
BET YOU DIDN'T KNOW THAT!

Check out these __________ (ADJECTIVE) facts about cheer- __________ (VERB ENDING IN "ING"):

- The first cheerleader is usually considered to be __________ (PERSON IN ROOM), who led the first organized __________ (NOUN) for the University of __________ (A PLACE) in 1898. In the beginning, cheerleading was a/an __________ (NOUN)-dominated field. In fact, the first __________ (VERB ENDING IN "ING") fraternity, Gamma Sigma, was all male.
- Recorded in (the) __________ (A PLACE) in August 2017, the largest cheer pyramid had sixty __________ (PLURAL NOUN) creating one __________ (ADJECTIVE) pyramid.
- On December 23, 2018, the largest cheerleading cheer was __________ (VERB (PAST TENSE)) in China by over __________ (NUMBER) people.
- There are more than __________ (NUMBER) cheerleaders in the US alone. Of those, 83 percent keep a/an __________ (LETTER OF THE ALPHABET) average, and 70 percent play a second __________ (NOUN).

MAD LIBS® is fun to play with friends, but you can also play it by yourself! To begin with, DO NOT look at the story on the page below. Fill in the blanks on this page with the words called for. Then, using the words you have selected, fill in the blank spaces in the story.

Now you've created your own hilarious MAD LIBS® game!

V-I-C-T-O-R-Y!

LETTER OF THE ALPHABET ____________________

LETTER OF THE ALPHABET ____________________

NOUN ____________________

SAME NOUN ____________________

NOUN ____________________

VERB ____________________

VERB ____________________

SAME VERB ____________________

ADJECTIVE ____________________

NOUN ____________________

VERB ____________________

PLURAL NOUN ____________________

VERB (PAST TENSE) ____________________

ADVERB ____________________

VERB ____________________

MAD LIBS®

V-I-C-T-O-R-Y!

Give me a/an ______________ (LETTER OF THE ALPHABET) and an *I*,

then give me a *C* and a *T*, a/an ______________ (LETTER OF THE ALPHABET), and an *R-Y*!

What's that spell? ______________ (NOUN)!

Say it again: ______________ (SAME NOUN)!

We've won the ______________ (NOUN), you had no chance!

We're going to ______________ (VERB) our victory dance!

So ______________ (VERB) us now, and ______________ (SAME VERB) us good;

we're the most ______________ (ADJECTIVE) team in the neighborhood!

Watch us hold the ______________ (NOUN) high.

It's time for you to ______________ (VERB) goodbye.

Pack our ______________ (PLURAL NOUN); get on that bus.

But you haven't ______________ (VERB (PAST TENSE)) the last of us!

Victory was ______________ (ADVERB) on our side.

It's time for you to ______________ (VERB) and hide!